# County Donegal Railways Bus Services
## Hugh Dougherty

E121 in Stranorlar Station yard, with a classic car of the period.

*Hugh Dougherty*

© Hugh Dougherty, 2023
First published in the United Kingdom, 2023,
by Stenlake Publishing Ltd.
www.stenlake.co.uk
ISBN 978-1-84033-954-3

The publishers regret that they cannot supply copies of any pictures featured in this book.

Printed by
P2D Books, 1 Newlands Rd,
Westoning, Bedford MK45 5LD

## Acknowledgements

This book is dedicated to the memory of the late Danny Boyle of Glenties, proud CDR clerical officer at Stranorlar, who taught the author everything he knew about CDR railway and buses and encouraged him on his many visits to CDR headquarters. Danny was an early preservationist, saving for posterity many CDR railway and bus artefacts, now on display at St Connell's Museum, Glenties, which he helped to found.

Thanks to Niall McCaughan, Donegal Railway Heritage Centre manager, Jim McBride, Donegal Railway Heritage Centre director, Paul Savage, Cyril McIntyre, all former CDR office staff, especially the late Maureen McGilloway, and bus crews.

The author is donating royalties from this book to the Donegal Railway Heritage Centre.

CDR man and preservation pioneer, Danny Boyle, in the Donegal Railway Room at St Connell's Museum. *Hugh Dougherty*

The notice which announced the end of the trains and the start of the buses.
*Hugh Dougherty*

# Introduction

When the County Donegal Railways Joint Committee reluctantly replaced its trains with buses in 1960, it transformed itself from the largest and best-known Irish narrow gauge railway, into a road transport organisation, but one that thought it was still a railway! The CDR rail replacement buses carried the same, eye-catching, red-and-cream livery as the trains they replaced and ran over the same routes to the same timetables. Behind their steering wheel and on the platform were former railcar motormen and guards, who had retrained as bus drivers and conductors. They ensured that the new, CDR buses, which proudly bore the railway's crest, continued to serve the public as best they could. They upheld the best railway traditions of the company, at that time jointly owned by British Railways London Midland Region and Coras Iompair Eireann, but fiercely independent, and very much part of the fabric of Donegal life. This is the story of these railway-owned buses, the crews who ran them, the passengers they carried and their almost inevitable take-over by CIE in 1971.

The County Donegal Railways Joint Committee crest carried on the trains and buses.
*Hugh Dougherty*

The 16 year-old author with a Tiger Cub at Stranorlar in July 1967, with a CDR lorry in the background. *The late Danny Boyle.*

On the Killybegs–Glencolumkille route bought from the Bogagh Bus Company in 1944, E124 waits its time near Glencolumkille in July 1969.

*Hugh Dougherty*

CDR bus in the landscape; An E class bus stops at Maas between Portnoo and Glenties, with Gwebarra Bay in the background. This was the original CDR bus route of 1930.
*Hugh Dougherty*

# County Donegal Railways Bus Services 1930-1959

If you arrived off the Ulster Transport Authority train from Belfast or Derry at Strabane in 1959, two County Donegal Railways Joint Committee, bright, red-and-cream, articulated diesel railcars, would have been waiting to take you onwards into Donegal over miles of 3ft gauge track.

In the goods yard, you'd have seen CDR wagons, headed by proud, red-liveried 2-6-4T steam locomotives, bringing goods that had arrived at Strabane over the broad gauge from Dublin, into Donegal.

Buses on rails: CDR railcar 12 of 1934, powered by a Gardner 6L2 engine, and built by Walker Bros of Wigan and the Great Northern Railway of Ireland, in action in July 1994 on the Foyle Valley Railway, towing its preserved sister, railcar 18 of 1936. Number 12 is currently a static exhibit in the Foyle Valley Railway Museum and 18 runs in the summer on the Fintown Railway, courtesy of its owners, the North West of Ireland Railway Society.

*Hugh Dougherty*

You might have concluded that this bustling, County Tyrone, junction was there to stay, with the CDR trains crossing the border into the Republic of Ireland, to Letterkenny, Stranorlar, Donegal Town, Killybegs and Ballyshannon, just as they had done for decades.

But, you'd have been wrong, for, in 1959, plans were well underway to consign the CDR trains to history, and replace them with buses and lorries. Time was fast running out for the CDR narrow gauge, as the company looked to the roads.

The CDR's involvement with buses, wasn't new, for the company, jointly owned by the Great Northern Railway of Ireland and the Midland Railway, later the London Midland & Scottish Railway, and, later still, by British Railways and Coras Iompair Eireann, had run buses from its Glenties railhead to Rosbeg, Portnoo and Maas in 1930.

The bus routes, instigated by the CDR's legendary manager, Henry Forbes, connected with trains at Glenties Station, but lost money. By 1933, the rough Donegal roads of the period had reduced the buses to scrap. The four, painted in the plum livery worn by the CDR's early railcars, were 1926-built Reos, new to United Motor Services of Tandragee, which had been taken over by the GNR(I), who sold the vehicles on to the CDR.

But, the redoubtable Henry Forbes, pioneer of railcars on the Donegal, and a real railway man, kept the two best buses, and converted them into railcars 9 and 10, in keeping with his drive to run his railway almost like a local bus service, with railcars stopping anywhere on request. Operated by the driver only, who sold tickets to passengers joining from the lineside, and dealt with mails, parcels and light goods, the railcars, virtual buses on rails, provided a flexible service, and kept the railway running until 1959.

Forbes did realise that private bus competition was starting to eat into CDR revenues. The situation became critical in the late

1920s and 1930s, when companies such as HMS Catherwood and Robert's of Londonderry, ran between the same towns as the railway, using lower fares to poach passengers.

The same was happening across Ireland, threatening rural railways, and, in Donegal the solution was to sit down with the Great Northern Railway of Ireland, joint owners of the CDR, already an established road passenger transport provider. In 1932, after extensive negotiations, which included defining the bus operating territories of the County Donegal Railways, the Great Northern and the Londonderry & Lough Swilly Railway, it was agreed that the GNR would operate bus services in the CDR area, closely integrated with the railway, on behalf of the CDR.

Known as the Donegal Area Joint Services, with routes, initially, between Derry and Ballyshannon, Donegal, Glenties and Portnoo, and Ballyshannon and Rossnowlagh, the joint services were operated under an agreement which apportioned the net revenue and loss or profit, at 80 per cent to the CDR and 20 per cent to the GNR(I). After Henry Forbes had died in post in 1943, and been replaced by Bernard L Curran as manager and secretary of the CDR, the joint services were expanded in 1944 to serve Malinmore from Killybegs, following the CDR purchase of the locally-owned Bogagh Bus Service, integrating the route with train times at Killybegs Station.

More services were added in 1946, with a route from Glenties to Dungloe, where the buses met the road passenger services of the Londonderry & Lough Swilly Railway. A new service, linking Letterkenny with Ballybofey, was instituted by Curran in the same year, allowing passengers to travel to and from Letterkenny without having to take the train to Strabane, joust with the Customs there and at Lifford, and change trains for Letterkenny. The CDR applied for and retained the licence for the new route, with GNR buses providing the service under the joint arrangement.

The direction of travel, towards buses and away from narrow gauge railway operations was clear, especially as the railway was starting to run at a loss, and needed large-scale track renewals, as traffic and revenue fell away following the boom years of the Emergency, as the Second World War was known in the Republic.

When the railway between Stranorlar and Glenties was closed to passenger traffic in 1947 because of worn-out track, the CDR again chose the GNR(I) to run the replacement buses on its behalf, with an enhanced service between Donegal and Glenties also being introduced.

The CDR railway and GNR joint bus services provided passengers with a well-integrated, local transport service, with trains and bus times arranged to allow transfers, and interavailability of bus and rail tickets as normal practice, passenger-friendly aspects of an integrated public transport service that many operators struggle to provide today.

The smart, well-run blue-and-cream GNR(I) Gardner and AEC Regal buses were a common site on Donegal roads, being parked at

One of the CDR's Reo buses which ran from 1930 to 1933 from Glenties Station. The bus is painted in the same plum livery as early CDR railcars.
*Paul Savage Collection*

GNR(I) Gardner bus 389, as used on the CDR-GNR(I) Donegal joint services. The bus is preserved in running order at the Cavan & Leitrim Railway's Dromod base.
*Hugh Dougherty*

CDR stations between runs and overnight, while the main GNR(I) garage was at Donegal Town, on land owned by the CDR, right beside the railway station. Despite being sparsely populated, then, economically depressed, largely cut off from its traditional trading hinterlands as a result of partition in 1922, and subject to large–scale emigration of young people, south Donegal enjoyed exceptional public transport provision, thanks to the foresight and enterprise of the CDR and GNR managements. Judicious use of buses, integrated with trains, also prolonged the life of the railway itself.

But change was in the air. The GNR(I) was in financial straits following the Second World War, and, as early as 1945, it proposed handing over its joint services in Donegal, entirely to the CDR, with the buses being painted in CDR livery and maintained at Stranorlar, but nothing happened. In 1953, a joint CDR and GNR(I) report, recommended that the CDR's entire narrow gauge railway should be closed and replaced with buses, with the Great Northern running the resulting, enhanced, bus services itself. In the meantime the GNR(I) was being wound up and taken over by the northern and southern governments under the Great Northern Railway Board, so, again, nothing happened.

But, the following year a new report emerged. Authored by Harry Patterson, GNR(I) Board accountant, with inputs from British Railways, owners of one half of the CDR, and Bernard Curran, it recommended that the CDR take over all bus services in its area. This would have suited Curran perfectly, while there was much local political and popular support for the idea, even though it was clear that the railway would be closed as part of the deal, but, again, no changes were made.

In the event, when the Great Northern Railways Board was wound up at the insistence of the Northern Ireland government in 1958, the Donegal Joint services were taken over by CIE, and still ran under the old agreement terms, jointly, with the CDR, which continued to run trains on the Letterkenny and Ballyshannon branch and its main line to Stranorlar, Donegal and Killybegs.

However, the CDR railway services were losing money hand-over-fist, with losses of £23,905 taking place in 1958, bringing the total loss from 1948 onwards to £137,000, and rumours began to circulate about the railway being closed. The *Donegal Democrat* reported in early 1959 that it understood that the railway would close on 30th September, and, as a result, Bernard Curran was summoned before Donegal County Council.

Curran clearly had a tough session, but he assured councillors that the railway would not close before 31st December and that the CDR was busy arranging replacement bus and lorry services, although he was unable to tell councillors who would actually run the buses. That was because no political decisions on the cross-border CDR had yet been taken in Dublin and Belfast, resulting in rumour and counter-rumour during what was a very worrying time for CDR and CIE joint bus service staff and management.

The *Donegal Democrat* speculated that the CDR would be wound up entirely, and that CIE would take over all operations in the county. Another rumour was that the Londonderry & Lough Swilly Railway, then highly-profitable, and operating bus and lorry services over its former rail routes to and from Derry and the north and west of Donegal, would be invited by the Republic of Ireland government to operate all services throughout Donegal. As the Swilly was headquartered in Derry, across the border in Northern Ireland, that put paid to this suggestion, the politics of partition impacting, as they have done frequently, on transport policy making in Donegal.

Despite this, the CDR had to prepare for the railway closure, hoping to absorb two-thirds of 157 staff employed on the railway into the replacement bus and lorry services. Contracts had to be issued, buses hired from CIE, if the CDR was to run the replacement services, timetables published, and agreement reached with northern and southern governments on the new arrangements.

Curran was forced to issue a public statement in November 1959, repeating the economic reasons for closing the railway, and admitting that although the CDR hoped to run the replacement bus services, with its own buses in its own livery, he was still unable to say so for certain.

It wasn't until 19th December, just weeks before the closure of the railway, that he issued staff with a circular – General Instructions – Omnibus Services – confirming the new arrangements.
The circular stated:

> The following routes will be operated by this Committee:
> 1. Strabane to Letterkenny, via Raphoe, Convoy, Glenmaquin and Lurgyback. Terminal points: Strabane- Railway Station (CDR), Letterkenny- Square
> 2. Strabane to Ballybofey via Castlefin (Diamond) calling at Liscooly and Killygordon. Terminals: Strabane- Railway Station (CDR), Ballybofey- Duncan's Café
> 3. Strabane to Killybegs via Castlefin (Diamond), Ballybofey, Donegal (Station and Diamond), Frosses and Dunkineely. Terminals Strabane- Railway Station (CDR), Ballybofey- Duncan's Café, Donegal- Breslin's Hotel, Railway Station, Killybegs- Railway Station
> The Donegal-Ballyshannon and Ballyshannon- Rossnowlagh Routes will be operated by CIE. [That was under the existing, joint Donegal services arrangements.]

By the end of 1959, then, the CDR was ready for the first day of rail replacement services on Friday 1st January 1960, and, despite the fact that the staff, public and politicians in Donegal were sorry to see the railway go, when the last train ran on 31st December, the changeover to buses was inevitable.

Despite press reports that the last passenger train's driver and fireman, Jim and Frank McMennamin, were in tears as they brought their historic train into Stranorlar, and where Bernard Curran was also overcome by emotion, it had been Mr Curran who had told councillors that the narrow gauge railway was outmoded, and that the company had been *"dissipating its energy over the last few years keeping it going."* He had also said that he hoped the new buses could recapture lost traffic and operate more cheaply than the railway. Time would tell.

The notice warning people to keep off the CDR private road between Strabane and Lifford, laid on the track of the Strabane & Letterkenny Railway. By 1968, the road was well out of use and the notice had seen better days, but the S&LR remained in existence as an legal entity until the CIE takeover in 1971.
*Hugh Dougherty*

A Donegal-bound E Class bus in the Barnesmore Gap with the railway trackbed on the hillside above. *Hugh Dougherty*

# County Donegal Railways Road Passenger Services 1960-1971

So it was, when the CDR withdrew its trains, that it replaced them with its own buses, over the same routes, and replicating the same timetables, on and from Friday 1st January 1960

But the buses faced their first challenge right away, and that was reaching Strabane Railway Station to connect with the Ulster Transport Authority trains on the former Great Northern 'Derry Road'.

The existing River Foyle road bridge was too weak to carry buses and lorries and CDR bus passengers had to alight at the Donegal side, cross the bridge on foot and climb aboard an Ulster Transport Authority bus, stop again for the British Customs, and get back on again to reach the station. The CDR crews were sorely tried, unloading passengers, luggage and parcels on and off the buses and meeting tight train connections while passengers complained bitterly.

The CDR acted immediately to solve the problem, lifting the track on the now-closed Strabane-Letterkenny line as far as Lifford, which included the CDR's own river bridge. The trackbed was tarred, and CDR buses and lorries then ran directly to and from Strabane Station, using the station platform at Lifford for Customs examination, before rejoining the public roads. This was real rail buses in action!

Railway enthusiast, Michael Bunch, travelled on the CDR bus from Strabane to Stranorlar in August 1960. He wrote of his journey on the tarred-over trackbed:

> I caught a bus to Stranorlar. It almost seemed as if it was a railbus as I went round the curve and over the bridge to Lifford, but I missed the noise of the metal wheels on rail joints and the clanking of the railcar's coupling rods.

The private roadway and bridge remained in use until the Foyle bridge was rebuilt by Tyrone and Donegal County Councils. CDR notices threatened dire penalties to anyone using their private roadway illegally.

The CDR ran its rail replacement buses in a railway-like manner, and in 1968, former railcar driver, Collins Lafferty, told the author:

> Yes, you had to remind yourself that you were now driving a bus, and that you had to steer it, unlike a railcar. That was especially true when you were on our road over the old Letterkenny line between Strabane and Lifford!

The railway kept the main stations open, basing buses and staff there, and the bus services, run from 1st January 1960, were operated by six 'P' class Leyland Tiger, single deckers, hired from CIE, painted in the CDR's distinctive railcar livery of red-and-cream, and proudly carrying the railway's crest.

A real rail bus! P174 stops at Lifford Station in 1961 for the Customs as the crew unload the heavy suitcases of the day. The Letterkenny bus has come over the CDR's own roadway from Strabane.   *S. J. Carse*

The buses had a sliding door, worked by conductors, while, like the railcars, they had roof racks and rear ladders. But, unlike the railcars they replaced, they had no heaters, leading to complaints from passengers and staff alike, before that was remedied.

In summer, 1960, a further four P type single deckers were hired from CIE, and all the buses were crewed by former railcar drivers and guards, trained through in-service training, before the changeover, for their new duties. There were 16 platform staff and one inspector, and the inspector mainly concentrated on traffic and promotional duties. The CDR bus services were blessed with excellent staff who put safety and public service foremost in the best traditions of the railway company, knew all their regulars, and played a vital part in the life of south west Donegal.

But the management did have its work cut out when the *Donegal Democrat* commented at the end of the first week's operations:

> Ireland's youngest road passenger transport service is in full operation this week, the CDR bus service covering most of County Donegal's labyrinthine network of roads in the West, South and East. So far everything is going smoothly and the management is on the 'qui vive' to iron out any problems that arise. The biggest snag that has arisen from the travelling public's point of view, however, is the big jump in fares, fifty per cent in most cases, but it would appear that nothing can be done about this as the increase was bound to come even if the rail service had continued.

The paper went on to report 'consternation' in Ballyshannon, where the mails that had previously arrived in the town by railcar, were now arriving much later by bus. And, by 26th February 1960, the paper reported that CDR buses were unable to operate through the Barnesmore Gap, between Stranorlar and Donegal Town, for four days, because of heavy snow, and commented that mail deliveries has been seriously affected.

The *Democrat* leader writer accused the CDR of being in a rush to close its railway and predicted a loss of post office contracts if it didn't do better, while it recorded that Reverend Father Cyprian, the Guardian of Rossnowlagh Friary, which, famously, had been provided with a special, Sunday railcar for Mass goers, regretted that the replacement buses did not run at time to suit Sunday Mass or the weekly St Anthony's Devotion on Tuesday evenings. In 1962, the *Democrat* was again after the CDR, when bus, P35, skidded on ice at Drumakillew near Inver, and was so badly damaged that it had to be scrapped, although the accident probably had more to do with the rudimentary road gritting of the day, rather than the driving expertise of the former railcar driver at the wheel. Not for nothing did the timetables carry the words:

> On occasions when snow or fog prevails, or the state of the roads is unusually difficult, it may be necessary to vary the times of the Omnibuses or to suspend the running of certain services without notice.

And, again, just to make sure that passengers knew what to do at the Customs, and didn't hold up buses by being caught smuggling, the same timetables warned:

> Passengers are personally responsible for declaration and clearance of all luggage, parcels etc, through Customs and are respectfully urged to have all baggage opened and ready for examination. Passengers failing to comply with the Customs Regulations render themselves liable to penalties under the Customs Acts.

Over the next few years, the new service settled down, with the buses running up an annual average figure of 240,000 miles, although the hoped-for profits and stable fares resulting from replacing the railway with buses did not materialise, thanks to falling passenger numbers and rising costs. On and from 1st January 1968, for example, fares were increased by 12.5 per cent, eight years after the buses took over from trains. That increase topped considerable annual increases from 1960 onwards.

## COUNTY DONEGAL RAILWAYS (JOINT COMMITTEE).

### ROAD PASSENGER SERVICES
### STRANORLAR – DONEGAL.

OPERATIVE AS FROM 2nd DECEMBER, 1 9 6 8.

**FARES LIST NO. 2**
**SINGLE FARES.**

| Miles | Stage | | | | | | | | | | | | Stage | | Stage | Fare |
|---|---|---|---|---|---|---|---|---|---|---|---|---|---|---|---|---|
| –    | 58 | Stranorlar/Ballybofey (58) | | | | | | | | | | | 59 | Stranorlar/Ballybofey | 58 | 5d |
| 2.0  | 55 | 10d | Filter Beds (55) | | | | | | | | | | 58 | Ballybofey/Derg Cross | 57 | 5d |
| 3.2  | 54 | 1/7d | 10d | Meencarrigagh N.S. (54) | | | | | | | | | 58 | Ballybofey/Doherty's Cross | 56 | 10d |
| 3.7  | 53 | 1/7d | 10d | 5d | McGroary's House (53) | | | | | | | | 44 | Cassidy's Lane/Donegal | 43 | 10d |
| 5.5  | 52 | 2/4d | 1/7d | 1/2d | 10d | Lough Mourne Bridge (52) | | | | | | | | | | |
| 7.8  | 51 | 3/1d | 2/4d | 2/–d | 2/–d | 1/2d | Derg Bridge (51) | | | | | | | | | |
| 9.9  | 50 | 3/11d | 3/1d | 2/9d | 2/9d | 2/–d | 1/2d | Callaghan's P.H. (50) | | | | | | | | |
| 10.4 | 49 | 4/3d | 3/6d | 3/1d | 2/9d | 2/–d | 1/2d | 5d | Barnesmore Halt (49) | | | | | | | |
| 11.2 | 48 | 4/8d | 3/11d | 3/1d | 3/1d | 2/4d | 1/7d | 10d | 5d | Barnesmore N.S. (48) | | | | | | |
| 12.6 | 47 | 5/1d | 4/3d | 3/11d | 3/6d | 3/1d | 2/–d | 1/2d | 1/2d | 10d | Lough Eske Stn. (47) | | | | | |
| 13.5 | 46 | 5/5d | 4/8d | 4/3d | 3/11d | 3/1d | 2/4d | 1/7d | 1/7d | 1/2d | 5d | Townawilly Cross (46) | | | | |
| 14.3 | 45 | 5/10d | 5/1d | 4/8d | 4/3d | 3/6d | 2/9d | 2/–d | 1/7d | 1/7d | 10d | 5d | Munday's Lane or Clar Church (45) | | | |
| 16.7 | 43 | 6/7d | 5/10d | 5/5d | 5/1d | 4/8d | 3/6d | 2/9d | 2/9d | 2/4d | 2/–d | 1/7d | 1/2d | Donegal Diamond (43) | | |

Fares please! A page from the CDR fares table for December 1968. Note that Barnesmore Halt is still used.   *Hugh Dougherty*

Outwardly, especially in summer, all looked well. Many parcels were handled, the roof racks would be piled high with luggage on busy days, keeping crews fit and agile shinning up the ladder at the back of the bus. They especially dreaded being hailed by a group of cycling, holidaying Christian Brothers, a savage teaching order, when up to 20, heavy, 1960's-style, bikes had to be hoisted up on to the roof rack, the good brothers, no doubt, hearing some unholy language from the crews….

The buses connected with the Belfast-Derry trains at Strabane and the CDR station's refreshment room, a popular haven for passengers arriving off the main line trains before going on to Donegal, became the subject of legal controversy in 1961. A new tenant applied for a licence, only to be refused, as the magistrate felt that the room was no longer served by trains, just buses. The case hung on whether or not it was still a railway refreshment room, the tenant arguing that it was, as the buses were operated by the County Donegal Railways Joint Committee, certainly not a mere bus company! He won his case.

Add to that the fact that, up until the demise of the Ulster Transport Authority, you could buy a through ticket to anywhere on the CDR bus routes to or from any railway station in the United Kingdom or Ireland, it was clear that the railway connection was strong. CDR conductors had to cope with collecting and cancelling through rail tickets, as well as issuing roll tickets from Setright registers, note the weather conditions and state of the roads, do a census of all passengers boarding and alighting at each stopping place, and record the name of the driver, still, as an echo of railcar days, given the grand title of 'motorman'. Filling up a CDR waybill and cashing in a mixture of money, vouchers and railway tickets was never easy.

What was remarkable was that the mighty British Railways London Midland Region, was joint owner of an Irish country bus heading west through the wilds of Donegal to Killybegs, driven by a former railcar driver in a CDR uniform, and doing its best to pretend that it was still a railway! If you looked hard in Euston Station in the early 1960s, you could even find a CDR bus timetable poster displayed near the booking office.

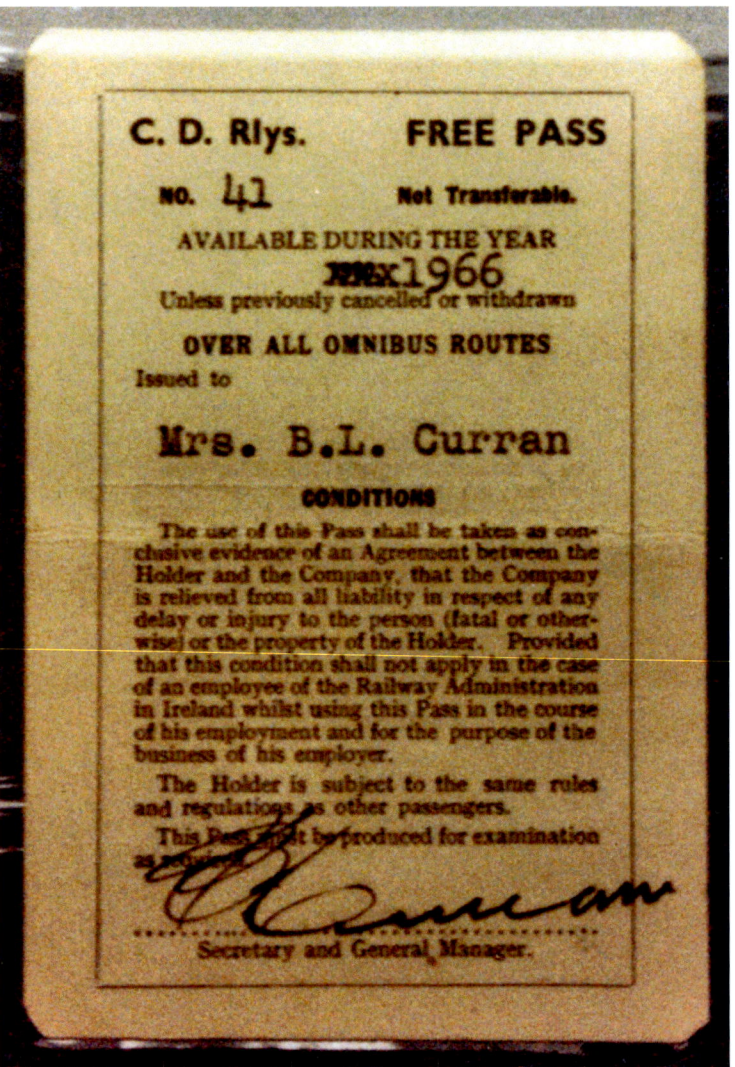

The free pass issued to Mrs Curran, the manager's wife.

*Hugh Dougherty*

## C.D.R.J.C. OMNIBUS SERVICES.

## CONDUCTOR'S WAYBILL.

Register No. [ ]   Depot .................... day of .................... 19....

Waybill Prepared By ....................

I have Checked the Opening and Closing Numbers of All Tickets enumerated on this Waybill also the Opening Numbers of Machine Counters Prior To Leaving Ticket Office and they agree with particulars recorded hereunder. .................... Conductor.

| Value Counters | | | | Value Of Tickets Sold | | | Passenger Counters | | | |
|---|---|---|---|---|---|---|---|---|---|---|
| | Closing Numbers | Opening Numbers | Difference (Units) | £ | s. | d. | | Single | Exchange | Total Tickets |
| Shillings Counter | | | | @ 1/- | | | Closing No. | | | |
| Half-pence " | | | | @ ½d. | | | Opening No. | | | |
| | | | | | | | No. of Issues | | | |

| Tickets Issued With This Waybill | | | | | | | Amount Paid In | | | |
|---|---|---|---|---|---|---|---|---|---|---|
| Description | Value | Closing No. | Opening No. | Opening No. of Tickets Returned | No. of Tickets Sold | | | £ | s. | d. |
| Booklet Tickets | | | | | | | Notes | | | |
| Through | — | | | | | | Silver | | | |
| Exchange Vouchers | — | | | | | | Copper | | | |
| Re-Book Vouchers | | | | | | | Total Cash | | | |
| Monthly Season | — | | | | | | Warrants | | | |
| Weekly Season | — | | | | | | Pre-Paid Vouchers | | | |
| Parcels Tickets | | | | | | | Rail Tickets | | | |
| Excess Fares | — | | | — | — | — | Fare Tickets | | | |
| | | | | Total | | | Total | | | |

A CDR waybill asked conductors for plenty of information, such as through rail tickets.

*Hugh Dougherty*

For that railway title was everywhere, as on wall timetables, carrying in large, bold, letters: 'COUNTY DONEGAL RAILWAYS JOINT COMMITTEE', with 'Road Passenger Services' added in a much smaller case, as though, if you looked elsewhere, there might still be a railway. That was also true of tickets, not forgetting the twice-yearly timetable booklet, featuring the railway crest on the cover, while CDR headquarters remained at Stranorlar, which proudly retained its station building with its characteristic clock tower.

In 1965, Bernard Curran was authorised to buy second-hand buses in England. CIE bus hire cost £50,000 annually, so, as a saving, the committee agreed to purchase its own buses for the basic service, but still hire CIE buses for summer traffic. There is no doubt that Curran regarded operating CDR buses in full livery, proudly carrying the railway's crest, as a statement of local control, and he made it the year before retiring, just as rumours of a CIE takeover began to spread. Stranorlar valued its independence.

After some consideration, the CDR settled on six ex-East Midland Road Car Company Leyland Tiger Cubs, with Saro bodies. The buses were new to the East Midland Road Car Co in 1954, each seating 44 passengers. They kept their English registrations, and ORR 321, 322 and 331 arrived in April, with 332, 333 and 339 coming in May. Stranorlar staff overhauled engines, gearboxes and running units, while O'Doherty of Strabane, the local coachbuilders, who had built railcar bodies for the CDR, as well as buses for the Londonderry & Lough Swilly Railway, refurbished the bodies.

Turned out in their red-and-cream livery, complete with railway crest, and the letters 'CDR' in the number screen box, they went into service straight away, with up to four CIE buses being hired to support them during the busier summer period. The author well remembers the brave sight in July 1965, of one of the class, complete with a full load of passengers, and sparkling in its new colours, speeding along the road to Donegal Town near Dunkineely. The CDR was alive and well, in the best traditions of the railway. Curran and the committee had made their point.

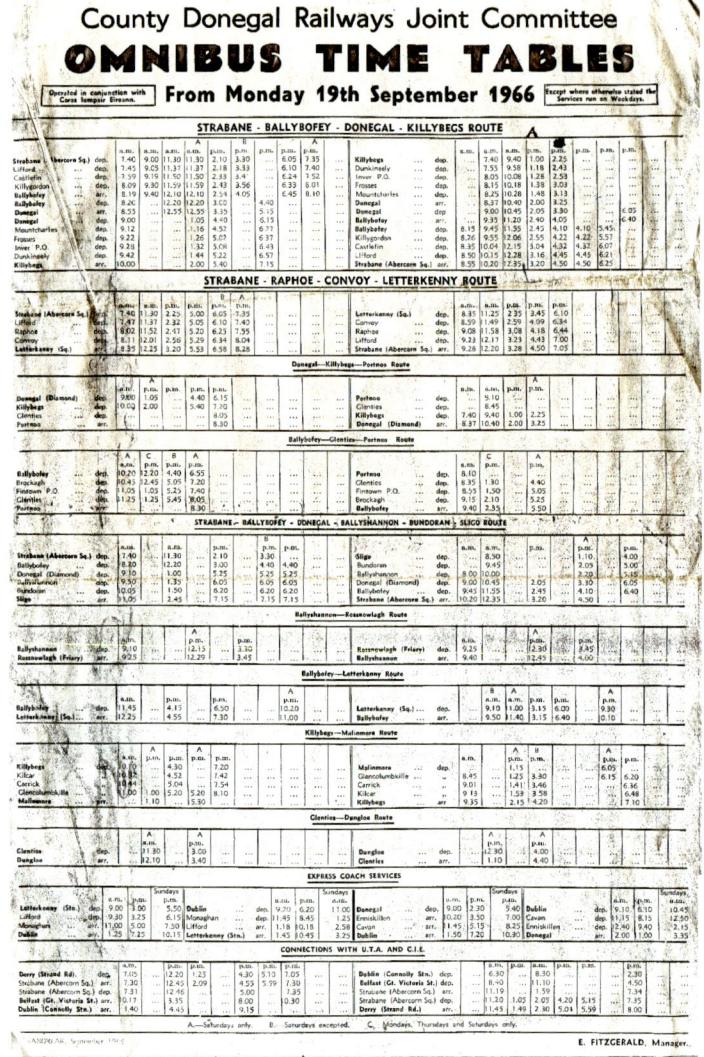

CDR wall timetable from September 1966, showing routes and connections.
*Hugh Dougherty*

The CDR headquarters, Stranorlar Station, built in 1863 by the Finn Valley Railway, still in use for bus, lorry traffic and as management offices in July 1966.
*Hugh Dougherty*

The cover of the day tours leaflet for 1965. *Hugh Dougherty*

These were good buses, although the crews found them a little too light for the then-punishing Donegal roads, and the traditional roof rack, which they lacked, was much missed when there was busy summer traffic off the Ulster Transport Authority Belfast-Derry express coach, which had replaced their trains in February 1965.

On those summer days, in the mid-sixties, during the North Twelfth holiday week, and, mid-July, when crews braced themselves for the Glasgow Fair traffic, bringing returning exiles and first and second generation, Glasgow-Donegal folk, who could present language difficulties and be just a bit wild, as many as three buses would head west into Donegal. Conductors had to make space on the Tiger Cubs using the front two rows of seats to accommodate suitcases, which of course, had to be taken off for the Customs, where passengers had to identify and open their luggage, and put it back on again. CDR crews had no sinecure operating across the border in those days, trying to keep time.

The Cubs served the CDR well, and, increasingly, with the demise of the 'P' buses, the then-new CIE 'E' class Leyland Leopards, came into the CDR fleet on hire. Built at CIE's Spa Road works in Dublin, they were excellent buses in every way, and much appreciated by crews. It was the late Mickey Lafferty, a former railcar driver who had gone on to the buses in 1960, who told me, as he drove his Leopard up the long gradient out of Stranorlar, and into the sunset, through the spectacular Barnesmore Gap, one fine July evening in 1968: "*The railcar was grand altogether,*" as he nodded over towards the abandoned trackbed. "*But these Leopards are almost as good.*" And he pushed his CDR uniform cap, which he had managed to keep, back up his forehead. That was praise indeed!

The CDR was generally profitable, with a few years of losses on the buses only, between 1960 and 1971. Profits on the road merchandise services easily carried the bus services, while the company chased every piece of traffic possible. That included a coach tour to Glencolumbkille, Sunday excursions to the seaside at Rossnowlagh, Bundoran and Portrush, and a flourishing private hire trade with Orangemen and members of the Ancient Order of Hibernians alike. But crews would be challenged severely as how to

*Below*: June 1968 handbill for Sunday excursions to Rossnowlagh and Bundoran. *Hugh Dougherty*

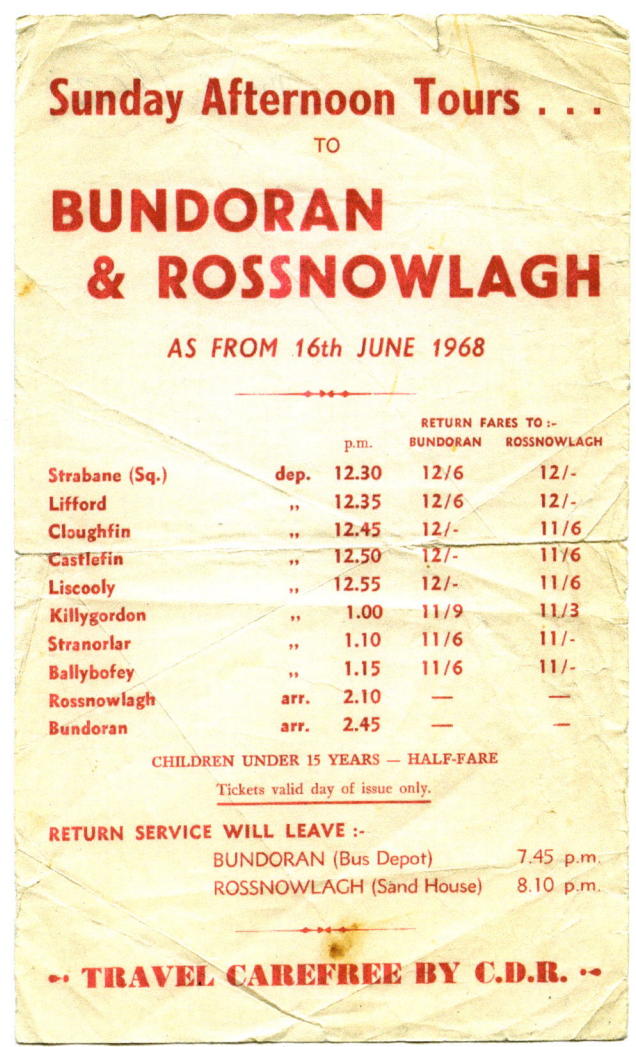

Day tours poster for 1970. *Hugh Dougherty*

load 40 Orangemen, one big drum and several banners into just one single decker. In railway days, there would have been a wagon attached to the railcar for the extras. Trains had their advantages.

Films for local cinemas were carried as parcels traffic. It was common to see a silver, metal box with a handle, plastered with CDR parcel tickets, containing the latest blockbuster for the Four Masters Cinema, awaiting collection, sitting on the pavement outside the bus office at the Abbey Hotel in Donegal Town as well as newspapers, while conductors picked up mail which went to Lifford sorting office, which was owned by the company. Some busy services needed duplicates, and the author well remembers the 6.15 pm joint-CIE service for Killybegs and Portnoo, leaving Donegal on a fair day, with a full load of West Donegal farmers and their families, one passenger even bringing a young calf he had just bought on board! Driver Mike Meehan didn't bat an eyelid, for he had seen it all before. This was a true country bus service in action. You won't find its like anywhere in Ireland or the UK today, and more's the pity.

But, all was not well, for, in 1966, the road passenger services made a record loss of £2,725. Wages and fuel costs kept rising and passenger numbers began to drop, as more and more Donegal folk bought cars, while the custom was also growing in Donegal of motorists giving locals lifts, so that fewer people used the buses.

By 1969, the buses had scraped their way back to a profit of £714 after three conductors were made redundant and one-man-operation was brought in, but not without a strike in 1967, which hit revenues over the summer. In any case, the CDR was beginning to fade away as an independent entity, for the writing was on the wall for Stranorlar rule.

British Railways, through the British Transport Commission, London Midland Region, had sold out its share of the CDR to CIE in 1966, and moves were afoot to wind up the CDR, despite the fact that the lorry services which delivered goods throughout Donegal from railhead at Derry and Sligo, were always profitable, and, in 1969, even allowing for a £4,446 loss on the bus services operated jointly with CIE, the whole undertaking had turned a profit of £29,392, a considerable sum by the values of the day.

A key event was manager, Bernard Curran's retirement in 1966, marked by a staff event and presentation to Mr and Mrs Curran in Jacksons' Hotel, Ballybofey. He was nominally replaced by E Fitzgerland, CIE's Galway area general manager, with day-to-day running of the CDR entrusted to Ricky Dunnion, CDR chief clerk, as chief executive officer at Stranorlar. Even though Mr Fitzgerald told the 140 staff attending the event:

I would like to assure CDR staff that no one was going to come from CIE with a big stick and start beating people over the head. There would be no radical changes that I can see necessary as the CDR is functioning efficiently as it stands.

In reality, though, CIE influence did come to be felt increasingly at Stranorlar. Out went CDR uniforms when they came up for replacement, and in came CIE issue clothing, as did CDR roll tickets, which were replaced by CIE standard tickets, although returns, seasons and parcel stamps remained the CDR's own until the end. And, with the closure of the 'Derry Road' railway through Strabane, in February 1965, the CDR abandoned its own station, and ran its buses up Railway Road to the town's Abercorn Square where connections were made with Ulster Transport Authority and, later, Ulsterbus services.

The last Tiger Cub was off the road by December 1970, and two, which had been hired to CIE for school bus work, for which the CDR had become responsible in its area, after free school transport was introduced by the Irish Government in 1967, had to be scrapped after rough treatment by school bus drivers. So it was that hired, CIE 'E' class Leopards, came to characterise the CDR in its final years. By this time, the buses operated in their CIE livery without CDR crests, and it was clear that CIE did not welcome replacing their logo with the CDR's own. It was a time of anxiety for all CDR staff, and a general meeting was held in Kee's Hotel in Stranorlar to explain what was likely to happen.

So, the end came on 12th July 1971, when, after legislation was passed in Dail Eireann and in the British Parliament, to rescind the

The end of the road for Tiger Cubs ORR 332 and 330 at Stranorlar in 1969. The station clock tower and footbridge were then intact, as are most of the railway buildings.

*Hugh Dougherty*

act of 1906 which had established the County Donegal Railway Joint Committee, CIE took over the CDR bus and road freight operations. On that day the usual CDR specials ran for the local Orangemen to take them to their demonstrations, but there was a general feeling of sadness and loss in Donegal at the end of a local institution and an efficient service, and a worry that control from remote Dublin would see services cut in the longer term.

The CDR did go down fighting, however, introducing express services to Belfast and Aldergrove Airport in conjunction with Ulsterbus, and, to the end, the management and staff were chasing new traffic, while the crews continued to run the buses in as railway-like a manner as possible. They knew their regulars, waited for them, passed the time of day, looked after school children and welcomed back exiles. It was a very personal service in the best traditions of the CDR.

The staff and buses transferred to CIE, and there was little sign of change for a few years. In 1974, however, CIE demolished the historic, CDR Stranorlar Station and ordered the last of several railway vehicles, including 2-6-4T *Columbkille*, two railcars, a carriage and a railcar red wagon, stored for preservation, off site. All were saved by the North West of Ireland Railway Society. The demolition was locally interpreted as CIE's desire to end independence in Donegal, although the state operator did want the site cleared to build a new bus garage, whereas the CDR had managed with the old station yard and facilities.

None of the Tiger Cubs survived into preservation, but two 'E' class buses, which were hired by the CDR, have. Leyland Leopard E152, the very bus that the author witnessed the calf travelling on, is beautifully restored by Dublin's Ian Molloy. It made a nostalgic trip to the Trail of the Rail Festival at Donegal Railway Heritage Centre in 2004, and ran an excursion to the Fintown Railway where its passengers enjoyed a trip on preserved CDR railcar 18, bringing the CDR's road and rail operations together once again.

E140 is preserved at the Cavan & Leitrim Railway at Dromod, while the dash panel of E121, the regular Stranorlar-Glenties bus of

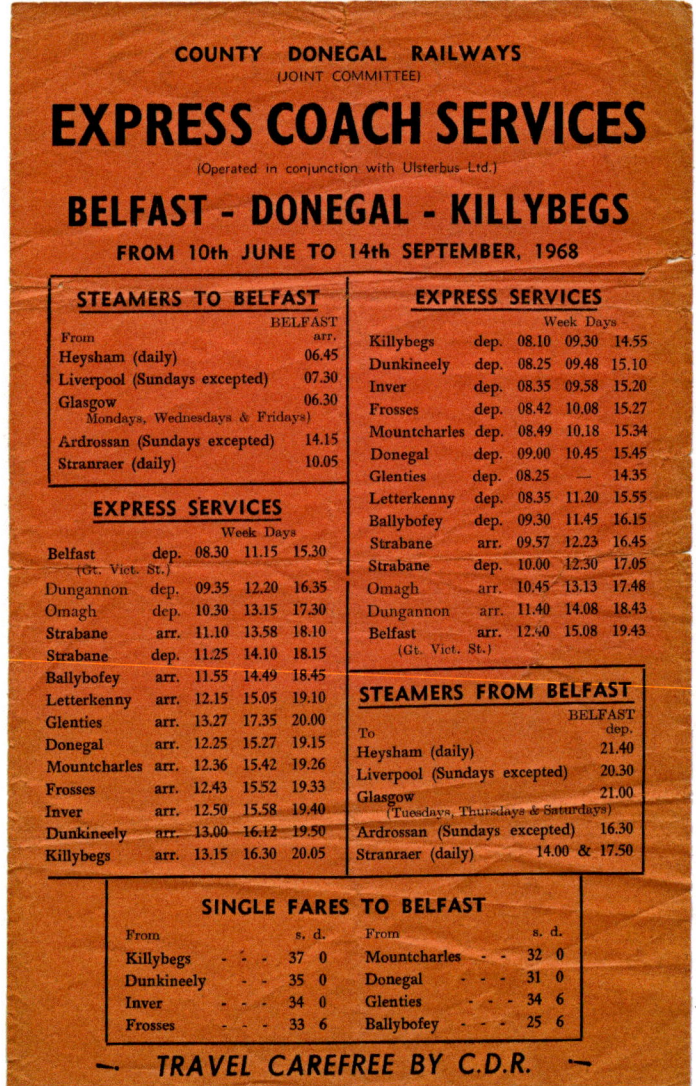

Bill for the new Belfast Express in 1970. *Hugh Dougherty*

The Belfast express loads at Donegal Diamond in July 1970. E169 was fitted with coach seats to boost passenger comfort. Former railcar driver, Collins Lafferty, is at the wheel, while his brother, Mickey, helps passengers board.

*Hugh Dougherty*

the mid-1960s, can be seen in St Connell's Museum in Glenties, along with a collection of CDR bus tickets and other railway artefacts.

There are bus timetables, ticket machines, fare tables and pictures at the most excellent Donegal Railway Heritage Centre, displayed, along with 2-6-4T *Drumboe* and items of rolling stock. Bus Eireann uses part of the station building for crew facilities, Donegal bus garage still stands, and Bus Eireann also uses the old CDR station at Letterkenny as the town's bus station. Sadly, the Lough Swilly, which out-survived the CDR, also used the station until 2014, when it ceased trading. Stranorlar, Bus Eireann, the successors to CIE, use the old CDR headquarters site as their central Donegal depot, and the station name board is on display along with the station clockfaces and a memorial to the CDR itself. It's doubly fitting that the entrance to the bus depot is in Railway Road as a link with the past.

And Oxford Diecast makes a 4mm scale model of CDR Tiger cub, ORR322. Resplendent in red-and-cream, carrying tiny CDR crests, it is Letterkenny-bound, the only item of County Donegal Railways rolling stock, rail or bus, to be produced in 'ready-to-run' model form. Its regular driver, the late Michael Galen, who drove railcars on the Letterkenny line, before transferring to the buses over the same route, would have been delighted.

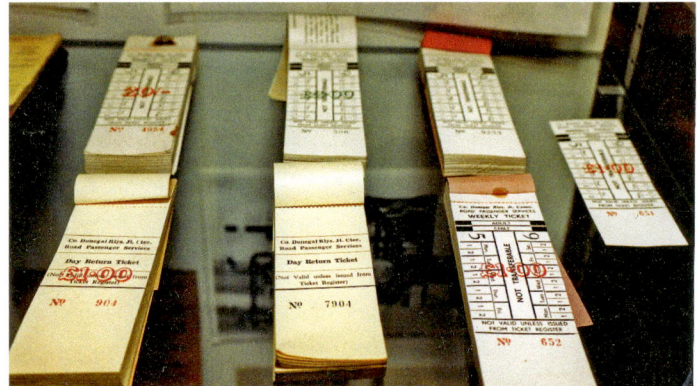

CDR bus tickets, in their original booklets, on display in St Connell's, Glenties. *Hugh Dougherty*

Today, Bus Eireann runs the former CDR routes. There are express services, buses offering a level of comfort undreamed of by CDR crews with their vehicles of the day, new passenger flows, such as heavy student traffic to and from bustling Letterkenny Institute of Technology, and faster running times, thanks to modern road building schemes. Few through passengers now come into Donegal via Strabane, once such a busy bus and rail interchange, the Customs have long gone, and most of the traffic for Donegal uses the busy Bus Eireann express routes to and from Dublin, Letterkenny and Donegal Town. It's worth wondering what CDR buses would have been like today, if the company had survived.

But the last word must go to the *Donegal Democrat*, often critical of the CDR, but, generally, supportive, and very much for local independence. Commenting on the final take-over by CIE in 1971, the paper's leader writer wrote:

The announcement which the '*Democrat*' carries exclusively this week, of the complete absorption by CIE of the CDR marks the end of an era in the history of Irish public transport. An old institution has gone forever. For many years, the CDR has been part of the lives of the people in two-thirds of the county of Donegal, and many will learn of its demise with a pang of regret. It served them well in the days when the service was confined to the railway, and, again, when it was transferred to the road. It was efficient service that it gave, and economical as well from the point of view of those who availed themselves of it.

The final act came, however, in January 1981, when the County Donegal Railways Joint Committee was dissolved by order of the Republic of Ireland Government. The committee had to be kept active to pay CDR pensions, before these were merged with the CIE scheme. The CDR as a legal entity, by then a railway company without a train, outlasted the buses, lorries and trains that it ran for 65 years between 1906 and 1971, by a further ten years. Henry Forbes and Bernard Curran would surely have approved!

Oxford Diecast model ORR 322 gets ready to leave for Letterkenny on the author's 4mm scale CDR railway layout. (Hugh advised the modelmakers on the details)
*Hugh Dougherty*

A CDR bus wash! The platform at Letterkenny Station was turned into a bus wash, simply by running the buses onto it, and hosing them down. ORR 331 has just been scrubbed clean.

*Hugh Dougherty*

The do-it-yourself bus wash at Letterkenny used the old station platform. ORR 331 is on it with a CIE container on a CDR trailer outside the old goods shed behind.
*Hugh Dougherty*

Down at Killybegs Station, former railcar guard, Tommy Kenny, then in charge at the station and relief driver, Peter Friel, stand in front of ORR 339 in July 1969.
*Hugh Dougherty*

# Bus Crews and Passengers

CDR buses went into service in 1960 with drivers and conductors. But, by the mid-sixties, conductors were on the way out throughout the bus industry, and, by 1971, when CIE took over, just two CDR conductors were still at work.

Now, with conductors long gone, it's worth looking at the CDR crews, saying who they were and what they did, long before driver-only buses, swipe card payment for fares, and internet booking.

The CDR conductors had been railwaymen, and brought the best of CDR traditions with them. Michael Boyle, for example, had been in charge of Lough Eske Station. He worked signals and points, issued train staffs to trains travelling through the Gap from Stranorlar to Donegal, and greeted passengers using his station. Michael went on to become road passenger inspector, while Danny Brannigan, who had been Joe Thompson's railcar guard on the Donegal-Ballyshannon branch line, also transferred to conducting after buses replaced trains. Danny, like Michael, finished his 46-year-long career as an inspector with Bus Eireann.

Conductors worked with former railcar drivers, turned bus 'motormen', as the CDR called them, such as Mickey Lafferty of Killybegs, his brother Collins, of Stranorlar, and Michael Gallen, who simply transferred from his railcar between Strabane and Letterkenny and drove his bus on the same route until he retired in 1988. By then, the CIE Road Passenger Services, which had taken over the CDR, had become Bus Eireann. When Michael died in 2019, he was the last former CDR railcar driver alive, and had known generations of passengers on his railcar and bus.

But the transition from railway to buses was no straight road, for, in 1959, the last year of the railway, no one seemed quite sure if the CDR itself would survive and, run the replacement buses, or whether CIE would take over the undertaking. There were local press rumours that the then-profitable Londonderry & Lough Swilly Railway Company, the CDR's great rival, and operators of buses and road freight in the north and west of Donegal, would absorb the CDR.

Jimmy McMullen shows how a CDR Setright ticket machine was handled as he takes his break at Strabane with Collins Lafferty, left, and storeman and relief driver Peter Friel, right, in July 1968. *Hugh Dougherty*

A CDR roll ticket from a Setright machine. *Hugh Dougherty.*

However, in anticipation of CDR buses taking over, railcar drivers were given in-service training to sit and pass their Public Service Vehicle Tests, and, as they operated over the border into Strabane, they had to hold licences for both the Republic and Northern Ireland, just as conductors had to as well.

Instructions for using the new ticket machines, were issued by the company accountant and conductors were told, in no uncertain terms, that they had to account for every single passenger on their bus, under pain of instant dismissal.

They also had to learn the current CIE Road Passenger Services Rule Book by heart, which, with some Great Northern Railway of Ireland bus forms, was adapted for CDR use. Conductors and drivers were tested on the rule book, in best railway tradition, before taking to the road.

Being a CDR conductor was demanding. Apart from issuing single, return and season tickets using the Setright Speed ticket machines, one of which is now preserved at Donegal Railway Heritage Centre, filling up a complex waybill, which recorded the state of the weather and name of the motorman, they had to deal with Ulster Transport Authority, CIE and British Railways through rail tickets to and from Donegal. They had to pick up, deliver to agents, and, sometimes, charge for parcels, affixing parcel stamps, and make sure that bundles of newspapers- with a free paper for the crew- were thrown off at shops en route, or transferred to another bus

In the summer there was lots of luggage, as many people still arrived in Donegal via Strabane, rail from Belfast until 1965, and the replacement UTA and Ulsterbus express bus services, after. The heavy and unwieldy suitcases of the 60s, and even family-sized, wicker hampers, not forgetting bicycles, had to be humped up onto the bus rook rack, if the bus had one. If it didn't, all had to be loaded in the back door of the Leyland Tiger Cubs, and, even on busy runs, some suitcases placed on the front two seats.

The real fun started when the bus reached Lifford Customs hut, for the conductor and driver had to unload the lot, have passengers identify their luggage, see it past the Customs men, load it back on, and, then keep time to make the Belfast connection at Strabane.

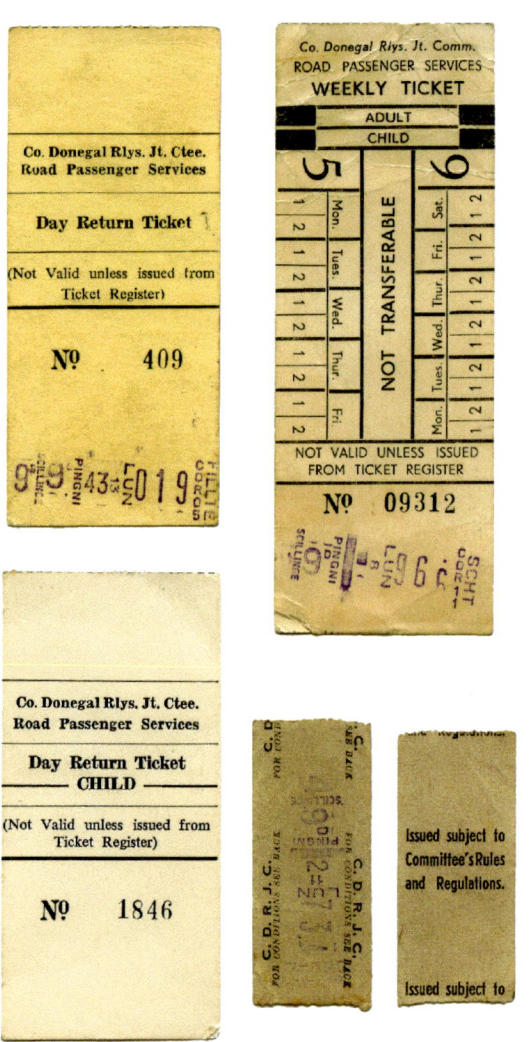

CDR season, single and return bus tickets.
*Hugh Dougherty*

E152 stops in Mountcharles on its way to Killybegs and Portnoo on the busy 6.15pm from Donegal Town in July 1970. On fair days a duplicate ran as far as Frosses.

*Hugh Dougherty*

It's July 1967, and ORR 321 is ready to leave Donegal Diamond for Killybegs.

*Hugh Dougherty*

Duplicate buses were common on busy days, and conductors would be stretched to the limit getting all their fares in, answering queries, and keeping the bus on time, while diving into CDR parcel agencies, such as Rule's shop in Killygordon, to drop off and pick up parcels. Many garages and farmers across Ireland and Britain waiting for spare parts, used bus parcels in those days to get their goods quickly, and the CDR did a brisk parcels trade in and out of and within Donegal.

In 1968, CDR crews dealt with parcels traffic worth nearly £3000, and £30,839 worth of fares passed through CDR ticket machines. It's worth remembering that this was long before inflation, the punt and the Euro.

Conductors accepted, and cashed-in Irish, English and Scottish and Northern Irish money, all of which circulated freely on both sides of the border. The biggest change was going decimal on Monday 15th February 1971, five months before the CIE takeover. For that, enough ticket machines had to be sent back to Setright to be altered in advance, although handling decimal cash made life much easier for both passengers, conductors, and by that time, drivers working One Man Operated, too.

CDR conductors also had to know their fare stages (some still used railway names such as Barnesmore Halt and Cavan Halt), and know that they could accept CIE-issued tickets on joint sections between Donegal Town and Ballybofey and Donegal and Killybegs.

Regular passengers were used to their bus stopping in the middle of the country and meeting another coming the opposite direction to allow crews to 'cross', as the CDR called it, borrowing the term from crossing trains at stations. A good example was the 18.05 Strabane-Ballybofey service, worked by a Strabane crew, which would cross with their Stranorlar-based opposite numbers near Liscooly Station. Both crews, then, got back home for the end of the day, avoiding expensive dead mileage. A crossing involved swapping CDR gossip and exchanging newspapers, before setting off back where they'd come from, with conductors, wearing ticket machine and cash bag, and with metal machine case in hand, also exchanging transfer slips to account for passengers.

Conductors carried and delivered company circulars, and internal mail, to and from Stranorlar headquarters and, as a friendly, local bus service, well-integrated into its community, urgent messages were often passed down the route to neighbours, on behalf of regular passengers.

There were occasional claims that CDR crews smuggled contraband over the border from Strabane, forbidden items such as copies of the *News of the World*, being carried in ticket machine cases, for distribution in Donegal, and, although a CDR lorry driver ended up in court for smuggling, no bus crews did. What is true, is that Strabane lie-overs between runs, allowed crews to shop for items cheaper in Northern Ireland. During the Troubles, the CDR did a brisk business in taking Donegal folk up to Strabane for bomb-damage sales held by shops there.

Despite riots in Strabane and Derry, CDR buses escaped damage, and few services were cancelled. Buying goods in Strabane, however, ran the risk of confiscation at Lifford Customs, and the author remembers an officer triumphantly seizing butter from the bag of a mother with a baby, because butter was then cheaper over the border than in Donegal. The crew had plenty to say about him as we went up the Finn Valley.

Sparkling Tiger Cub, ORR 339 and P class Leyland P353, stand outside Strabane Station in July 1967. *Oxford Diecast.*

In 1968, a CDR conductor earned just under £1,000 per year, and a driver, around £1,100, the industry's then going rate, and a good wage in a rural area. CDR bus crews benefitted from a steady job, paid holidays, a smart uniform and railway privilege tickets for train travel in Ireland and the UK, as the CDR was still a railway company, even if it had no trains after 1960!

Crews worked a six-day week, with Sundays off, although regular excursion work in summer, to Bundoran and Rossnowlagh, from Strabane and Killybegs, offered seasonal overtime. The Strabane crew would book on to leave at 12.30, a time chosen to give locals plenty of time to attend Mass(!), call at Lifford at 12.35, Cloughfin at 12.35, Castlefin at 12.50, Liscooly at 12.55, Stranorlar station at 13.10 and Ballybofey at 13.15.

A fast run took place through the Barnesmore Gap and Donegal, to Rossnowlagh, where passengers were dropped at the Sand House Hotel, for the magnificent strand, pictured on CDR leaflets, at 14.10. Bundoran pleasure seekers arrived in the Atlantic resort at 14.25 and decamped to the beach, the Bargain King, the amusements or, on wet days, the shelters up by Rougey Rocks.

The bus or buses, depending on demand, parked at Bundoran CIE depot, the old railway station site, and crews would be free until 19.45. They would enjoy a high tea before departure, after taking the Atlantic air. In good weather, some even took the plunge in Bundoran's surf, or, if wet, stayed at the bus office, swapping tales with the CIE, Erne Bus Service and Ulsterbus crews, whose excursion buses also parked at the station. Then, it was hell-for-leather for Rossnowlagh, to pick up non-stop for Ballybofey, and up the Finn Valley to Strabane, dropping off sun-burned and happily-exhausted families, before sweeping out the bus and booking off around 22.00. On Monday morning they would start all over again with the 07.40 departures for Killybegs and Letterkenny. It could be hard going, as one of Collin's Lafferty's grown-up sons, who became a doctor in Dublin, told the author: *"We didn't see much of him in the summer. He was always working very hard on the buses."*

School pupils also kept crews busy. Before 1967, when free school transport was introduced in the Republic, pupils used service buses,

Booklet timetable from 1967. *Hugh Dougherty*

Tiger Cubs ORR 331 and 321 in run-down condition at Stranorlar, and ready for withdrawal in 1970. A CIE schools service Bedford, in passenger livery, hired in from CIE, is to the left, and the old railway sheds are behind.
Hugh Dougherty

and paid fares to schools in Donegal, Stranorlar, Raphoe and Letterkenny, and a school duplicate ran from Killybegs to Donegal Town. Pupils could be quite lively at times, with crews keeping order on the bus!

Two new routes were introduced for schools in 1968, Porthall to Raphoe, and Porthall to Strabane. The services were not listed in public timetables, but locals used them, and, although unofficial, the routes appeared in fare tables issued to conductors.

As general manager Bernard Curran reminded his new bus crews in his December 1959 circular, with definite shades of predecessor manager Henry Forbes' exhortations to his then-new railcar crews of the 1930s:

> You depend, as the company depends, on public support. By winning and keeping public goodwill, you not only make the performance of your duties more pleasant, but you make the company prosper, and so help to ensure your livelihood. Efficiency brings reward in due course, though the good conscience that comes of duty well done may appear adequate reward in itself.

E154, and another E class bus, stand at Strabane's Abercorn Square terminus during the last week of operation, before CIE took over on 12th July 1971.
*Hugh Dougherty*

By 1967, however, chill winds were beginning to blow around the CDR buses, as more private cars came on to the Donegal roads, travel habits and routes into Donegal changed, costs rose, and passenger numbers fell. The push was on to retrain drivers to work one-man, OMO, as it was known then, and, yes, the CDR crews were all male in those days!

That caused a strike in July 1967, during the busy holidays. Michael Gallen was ordered to operate a Saturday evening, Letterkenny run without his conductor, and the 16 bus staff, National Association of Transport Employees members, struck. After a week's impasse, the strike made local and national press, valuable revenue was lost with the cancellation of all services, including the popular excursions to Rossnowlagh and Bundoran. Negotiations started after the men agreed to return to work, but it was clear what was coming. By the 1971 CIE takeover, there were two conductors left, Danny Brannigan and Michael Boyle, with OMO the norm on most routes.

CDR conductors and drivers were obliging, friendly, much valued by their passengers and excellent ambassadors for Donegal, when meeting people transferring on to CDR buses at Strabane, often welcoming back returning exiles on holidays. They were very conscious that the County Donegal Railways Road Passenger Services were much more than just a bus service. They were RAILWAY men, with railway heritage and tradition, and, especially, a commitment to passengers, easily transferred from rail to road.

But what of the passengers? The CDR buses, at the start of the 1960, carried many of the people who had used the railway, the best-known being a solicitor who lived in Stranorlar and who had travelled by train daily, for 40 years, to his office in Strabane. He became a bus regular on the same route.

There were Finn Valley housewives shopping in Strabane, folk travelling to shops in Letterkenny and to the Donegal County Council offices in Lifford. Crews knew all their regulars, conductors often asking them, to promote excursions: "Are you coming to Portrush or Bundoran with us this weekend?"

Convoy Woolen Mills workers [with one l in woollen], soldiers for Finner Camp and Franciscans for the Friary at Rossnowlagh,

Former railcar driver Mickey Lafferty, and now busman, stands proudly in front of his Tiger Cub, ORR 321, at Donegal goods shed in July 1967.
*Hugh Dougherty*

The replacement buses reversed under the railway bridge beside Friary Halt at Rossnowlagh to return to Ballyshannon. *Hugh Dougherty*

returning 'Yanks' and 'Scotchies' on holidays, all used the buses. The author remembers a travelling, Hungarian spectacle seller on Mickey Lafferty's Killybegs bus, trying to sell passengers a pair of glasses!

Passengers and crews crossed themselves when passing a Catholic Church, and Mike Meehan, on the Donegal-Portnoo CIE joint service, was spotted by the author in 1966, issuing a ticket to a women on the platform, changing smoothly from first into second gear on an E class Leopard- no mean feat- steering, and blessing himself all at once while passing the church in Ardara. That was a CDR miracle…

You would meet native Irish speakers on remoter routes, especially around Fintown, asking for their fare in Irish, although the CDR never had Irish language timetables or notices. Bus destination blinds were in English, even though CIE adopted Irish blinds to mark the 50th anniversary of the Easter Rising in 1966, and some hired CIE buses did retain Irish language blinds on CDR service.

Holidaymakers arriving in Derry off the 'Scotch Boat" from Glasgow, used the CIE and CDR joint services to reach places such as Portnoo and Killybegs, while others would come via Strabane, or use the Sligo-Derry service. Many would travel to Letterkenny from Strabane to connect with Londonderry & Lough Swilly Railway services for places such as Burtonport and Gweedore. These were epic journeys, especially for children, when distances seemed longer than today and getting to Donegal was more of an adventure. The last section home to Donegal and the first section on the way back, was by CDR or Lough Swilly bus, as the author well recalls.

The CDR buses were an essential link in keeping Donegal connected, and the booklet timetable contained several pages of through connections, by CDR bus, then, rail and boat, to Glasgow, Birmingham and London homes, to the Donegal diaspora.

It was vital to keep to the timetable and lose no time, then at Ballybofey, when transferring passengers from the Glenties bus, on to the Strabane service, to ensure that these CDR travellers made their connections on from there, to reach their destinations so far from the homes and hills of Donegal.

The clock faces from the Stranorlar Station tower were saved and erected in 2000 outside the Bus Eireann depot built on the site of the station, along with a memorial to the CDR.
*Hugh Dougherty*

ORR 331, parked in Stranorlar Station yard in August 1968.

*Hugh Dougherty*

Hired from CIE, E154, takes a break outside Killybegs Station in July 1968.

*Hugh Dougherty*

E121 has just left Stranorlar Station, on the right, for Ballybofey to take up service to Glenties and Portnoo in July 1969.     *Hugh Dougherty*

E121 in its prime, as passengers board for Glenties and Portnoo in Ballybofey in July 1969

*Hugh Dougherty*

# Road Merchandise Services

The railway ran 34 lorries and trucks, 4 tractor units and 14 trailers in 1960, and earned £123,503 from the service which replaced goods trains. Freight was collected from trains at Strabane and Sligo, for distribution around Donegal. Two tankers were maintained for the Killybegs fishing fleet fuel oil contract and a CDR lorry left Killybegs each night with fish for the Dublin markets. Two drivers were employed and took a pride in reaching the market early to get the best prices for their fishermen. A mail and express parcels van also ran the length of the county daily.

With the closure of the railway through Strabane in 1965, CDR lorries went to Waterside Station goods yard in Derry, where they transhipped goods for Donegal which had come from Dublin. CDR lorries were based round the county at Stranorlar, Letterkenny, Donegal Town, Glenties and Killybegs, and the railway goods sheds remained in use at Stranorlar, Donegal, and Letterkenny, with the station-based lorries serving their hinterlands.

The fleet included Leyland Comets and Albion tractor units, with Ford Thames mail and parcel vans. All lorries and vans were painted in CDR red and cream livery and were branded 'CDR'. They were maintained at Stranorlar, although after CIE influence was extended from 1966 onwards, repaints were done in CIE black, but still with the letters 'CDR' prominent.

In 1969 CDR road freight vehicles ran over one million miles, and made a profit of £21,092. They carried £124,170 worth of general merchandise, £34,355 of minerals, £14,422 of mails, £6,116 of parcels, £395 of coal, and £301 of livestock. Traffic could be booked in and out of Donegal via Northern Ireland Carriers, CIE and British Railways, and freight for western parts of Donegal was transferred to Lough Swilly lorries at Letterkenny.

Many former railwaymen were employed, such as Jim McMennamin, one of the last steam drivers at Stranorlar, who drove the last CDR passenger train. Jim stayed on as a Stranorlar lorry loader, and was always ready and delighted to tell interested visitors about his 40 years on the footplate. Joe Thompson, the former regular driver of the Donegal-Ballyshannon railcar, transferred to the goods shed at Donegal, so that the railway tradition was alive and valued in the road freight section.

All CDR road freight vehicles, drivers and helpers, were transferred to CIE on 12th July 1971, along with the buses and assets of the CDRJC and Strabane & Letterkenny Railway.

*Left*: In 1968, the CDR was chasing traffic by advertising in the Irish Press.
*Hugh Dougherty*

---

**County Donegal Railways**
(JOINT COMMITTEE)

**ROAD PASSENGER SERVICES**
Express and local services operated in conjunction with Coras Iompair Eireann.

**ROAD FREIGHT SERVICES**
Modern fleet of vehicles and containers—Working arrangements with Shipping Companies at Derry and Belfast Ports—Express Freight Service for Unit Loads or small consignments to and from Dublin and other centres in the Republic of Ireland.
Our representative is available to discuss your requirements.

E. FITZGERALD,
Manager.

STRANORLAR.
Phone Ballybofey 8 (2 lines).

A CDR Leyland lorry at the goods store in Stranorlar Station yard in July 1966, with Stranorlar East signal cabin. Lorries used the old railway facilities until a new goods shed was built. Today, this area is under new housing on what is called Railway Road.   *Hugh Dougherty*

A real, rural bus terminus! An old gate and an iron bed end kept Leyland Leopard E152, the regular Portnoo-Donegal Town bus secure between runs in 1968.
*Hugh Dougherty*